American Slavery and
the Fight for Freedom

RESISTANCE TO SLAVERY

FROM ESCAPE TO EVERYDAY REBELLION

Cicely Lewis

Lerner Publications ◆ Minneapolis

LETTER FROM CICELY LEWIS

Dear Reader,

Growing up, I learned about Black history only in February. There was a small section in our history textbook about slavery, and then we discussed the Civil Rights Movement. That was it. I always wondered about my ancestors. Did they fight back? How could someone own another human being? What happened between slavery and the Civil Rights Movement?

Cicely Lewis

Then I went to college and took an African American literature class. My whole world opened up as I learned about my history. I started researching and seeking more information. Looking back, I felt like I had been tricked. Why hadn't I learned these things sooner?

As an educator, I want to make sure my students never feel this way. I want you to know:

- Black history didn't begin with slavery.
- Neither Abraham Lincoln nor the Civil Rights Movement ended racism.
- Black people have always fought back.

I want to share the strength, power, *joy*, complexity, and beauty of Black history. This is the gift I hope to give you with this series—but don't stop here. Seek out knowledge wherever you go and question everything.

Yours in solidarity,

—Cicely Lewis, Executive Editor

TABLE OF CONTENTS

Think critically about the photos and illustrations throughout this book. Who is taking the photos or creating the illustrations? What viewpoint do they represent? How does this affect your viewpoint?

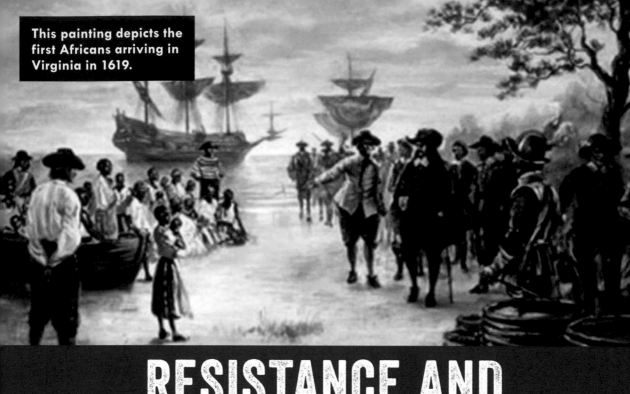

This painting depicts the first Africans arriving in Virginia in 1619.

RESISTANCE AND REBELLION

IN 1619 A GROUP OF ENSLAVED AFRICANS ARRIVED IN BONDAGE TO THE ENGLISH COLONY OF VIRGINIA IN NORTH AMERICA. At the time, the United States did not exist. Slavery would have a great role in shaping the US. According to the 1619 Project, a journalism project that aims to reframe US history and emphasize the place slavery and resistance had, "No aspect of the country that would be formed here has been untouched by the 250 years of slavery that followed."

Over 250 years, millions of Africans were brought to North America, South America, and the Caribbean to work as enslaved people. Hundreds of thousands of Africans were brought to America.

Slavery was rooted in white supremacy, the belief that white people are a superior race. It was a system to keep enslaved people oppressed. Enslaved people suffered unspeakable hardships. But they resisted.

Throughout the history of slavery, Black people found ways to fight back, whether it was through everyday

Many enslaved people did hard labor, such as picking cotton, on plantations.

On August 28, 1963, thousands of people participated in the March on Washington to protest for equal rights for Black people.

acts, rebellions, or escape. But even after slavery was abolished, Black people continued to be treated unequally during the Jim Crow era, a period of time where laws were made to limit the rights of Black people. Black and white people were segregated, and Black people had to continue fighting for their rights. The fight still goes on. Time and again, Black people have shown strength and courage to overcome oppression.

"African Americans during slavery, after slavery, during Reconstruction, during Jim Crow and after Jim Crow, and some would say into the new Jim Crow, have always tried to decide as much about our fate as possible."

—Alaine Hutson, history professor at Huston-Tillotson University

A Black Lives Matter protest march in New York City in 2020

Black people in front of their housing on a plantation in Beaufort, South Carolina, in 1862

CHAPTER 1
EVERYDAY RESISTANCE

NO HUMAN SHOULD OWN ANOTHER HUMAN. But enslaved people were considered the property of their enslavers. Enslaved people had few rights. They were not allowed to own property, to read or write, and more. Some participated in rebellions to fight for their freedom. Others participated in everyday acts of resistance.

Resistance to slavery began early on among Black people. At ports on the West African coast, African captives resisted by running away. Aboard ships, Africans mutinied. Sometimes they cast themselves into the ocean in resistance. After arriving in America, some Africans ran away. They looked for refuge among Native Americans and formed communities.

Enslaved people lived and worked in horrible conditions. Many worked from sunrise to sunset in the fields on plantations. They did hard labor under the hot sun and did not receive enough food or water to stay healthy. Other

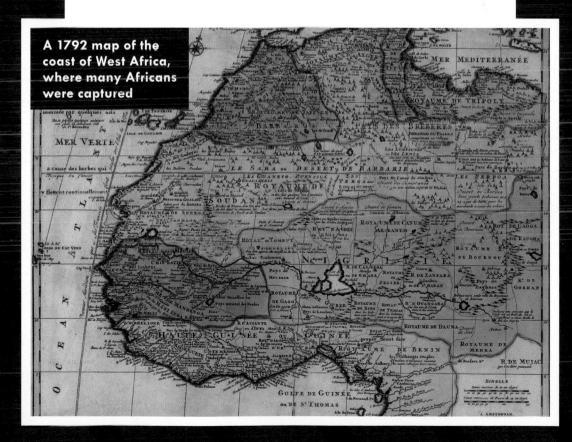

A 1792 map of the coast of West Africa, where many Africans were captured

"The greater part of the plantation owners were very harsh if we were caught trying to learn or write. . . . We were never allowed to go to town and it was not until after I ran away that I knew that they sold anything but slaves, tobacco, and whiskey. Our ignorance was the greatest hold the South had on us. We knew we could run away, but what then?"

—John W. Fields, former enslaved person, aged eighty-nine

enslaved people worked in enslavers' homes as house servants. Enslaved women cooked, cleaned, and took care of their owners' children. House servants were often watched closely by those who owned them.

At night, enslaved people returned to their housing. These shelters did little to protect them from harsh weather. Enslaved people rarely received proper medical treatment when sick. Many suffered from malaria, a deadly disease. Enslaved people were often required to work even when ill. They could be beaten, whipped, sold away from their families, abused, and murdered.

To fight back, they engaged in day-to-day resistance. They broke tools, learned to read, faked illness, and slowed down work. Meanwhile, laws were enacted to prevent enslaved people from rebelling.

THE DEPTH OF BLACK HISTORY

Black history does not begin or end with slavery. African kingdoms, such as the Ghana and Songhai empires, existed thousands of years before American slavery. These kingdoms had their own art, cultures, and economies. Black history is full of people you may have never heard of such as US deputy marshal Bass Reeves, American Revolutionary War hero Crispus Attucks, and the millions of Africans who lived before, during, and after American slavery.

Phillis Wheatley was an enslaved person who learned to read and write and became a published poet.

South Carolina.

At a General Assembly begun to be holden at Charles Town on the sixth of November in the thirteenth year of the Reign of our Sovereign Lord George Second by the grace of God of Great Britain France and Ireland King Defender of the and in the year of our Lord one thousand seven hundred and thirty nine and from continued by divers adjournments to the Tenth May one thousand seven hundred and forty.

An Act for the better Ordering and Governing Negroes and other Slaves in this Pro

Whereas in his Majesty's Plantations in America Slavery has been introduced and allowed; And the People commonly called Negroes Indians Mulatoes and Mestizos have been deemed absolute Sla and the Subjects of Property in the hands of particular Persons the extent of whose power over such Sla ought to be settled and limited by positive Laws So that the Slave may be kept in due Subjection and obee and the owners and other persons having the care and Government of Slaves may be restrained from exercising too great Rigour and Cruelty over them and that the Public Peace and order of this Province m preserved We pray your most Sacred Majesty that it may be Enacted c And Be it Enacte the Honble William Bull Esquire Lieutenant Governour and Commander in Chief by and with the a and Consent of his Majesty's Honble Council and the Commons House of Assembly of this Province and

The Negro Act of 1740 passed after the Stono Rebellion.

CHAPTER 2
REBELLIONS

ALTHOUGH MOST ENSLAVED PEOPLE RESISTED SLAVERY IN SMALL, EVERYDAY WAYS, SOME TOOK PART IN REBELLIONS. One of the largest rebellions was on September 9, 1739. A group of enslaved people gathered at Stono River in the colony of South Carolina to plan their escape to freedom. The group took control of a store, grabbed weapons, and killed the shopkeepers. Then they killed white homeowners and burned buildings.

Enslavers caught up to the group, and many were killed. In response to the Stono Rebellion, South Carolina passed a law called the Negro Act of 1740. The act limited the rights of enslaved people. They were no longer allowed to assemble in groups, earn their own money, or learn to read.

An enslaved man named Gabriel Prosser was inspired by the American, French, and Haitian revolutions because of their ideas about freedom. He planned to go to Richmond, Virginia, and hold Governor James Monroe hostage until enslaved people in Virginia were set free. Gabriel expected

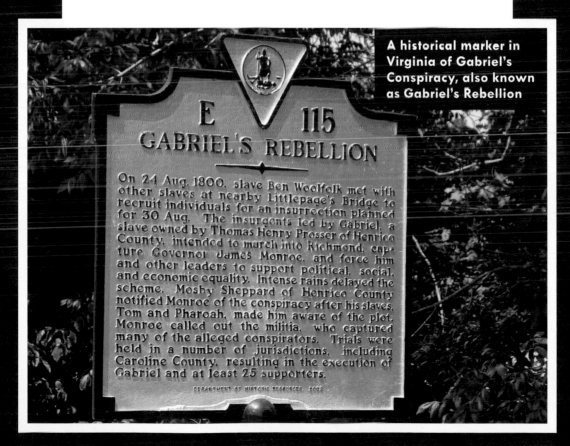

A historical marker in Virginia of Gabriel's Conspiracy, also known as Gabriel's Rebellion

E 115
GABRIEL'S REBELLION

On 24 Aug. 1800, slave Ben Woolfolk met with other slaves at nearby Littlepage's Bridge to recruit individuals for an insurrection planned for 30 Aug. The insurgents led by Gabriel, a slave owned by Thomas Henry Prosser of Henrico County, intended to march into Richmond, capture Governor James Monroe, and force him and other leaders to support political, social, and economic equality. Intense rains delayed the scheme. Mosby Sheppard of Henrico County notified Monroe of the conspiracy after his slaves, Tom and Pharoah, made him aware of the plot. Monroe called out the militia, who captured many of the alleged conspirators. Trials were held in a number of jurisdictions, including Caroline County, resulting in the execution of Gabriel and at least 25 supporters.

DEPARTMENT OF HISTORIC RESOURCES, 2002

one thousand enslaved people to join him, but a huge storm arrived on August 30, 1800, the day of the planned attack.

The plan was delayed, and a few enslaved people told enslavers of Gabriel's plan. Gabriel and several other enslaved people were arrested and executed. As a result of the rebellion, called Gabriel's Conspiracy, white people increased restrictions on the enslaved.

Nat Turner's rebellion is one of the most well-known uprisings. On August 12, 1831, Turner and his followers killed about sixty white people before being captured and killed. The rebellion caused much fear among white people. About two

REFLECT

How can resistance lead to change, and what does resistance mean to you?

hundred Black people, many of whom were not involved in the rebellion, were murdered by white mobs.

Joseph Cinqué, also known as Sengbe Pieh

Although the importation of enslaved people to the US was banned in 1808, it was not banned elsewhere. In 1839 the Spanish ship *Amistad* left Cuba carrying enslaved Africans. While at sea, the fifty-three Africans on board were led by Joseph Cinqué and rebelled, took control of the ship, and demanded to be brought back to Africa.

Instead, the *Amistad* docked in the US and a legal battle began. Cubans wanted the Africans to be returned to them. The case went to the US Supreme Court and ended in victory for the Africans. In 1841 they returned to the area now known as Sierra Leone.

Many people died during uprisings. Whether successful or unsuccessful, the rebellions paved the way for the abolitionist movement and the Civil War.

Many enslaved people escaped slavery with the Underground Railroad, as shown in this 1893 painting by Charles T. Webber.

CHAPTER 3
THE JOURNEY TO FREEDOM

WHEN ENSLAVED PEOPLE ESCAPED, SOME JOURNEYED TO THE NORTH FOR FREEDOM. Many others purposely ran only short distances away as a means to halt work on plantations. Escape attempts were dangerous and uncertain. Still, many enslaved people fled to freedom with the help of the Underground Railroad.

The Underground Railroad was a network of people, or conductors, who used their homes and businesses, or stations, to help guide enslaved people to freedom. Enslaved people moved from station to station until they reached free territory. Harriet Tubman is one of the most well-known heroes of the Underground Railroad. She was responsible for leading many enslaved people to freedom. But many others helped those on the Underground Railroad as well.

David Ruggles was born a free Black man near Norwich, Connecticut. He found safe passage to the North for many enslaved people, including a man named Frederick Bailey. Later, Bailey became known as Frederick Douglass, a well-known author and abolitionist.

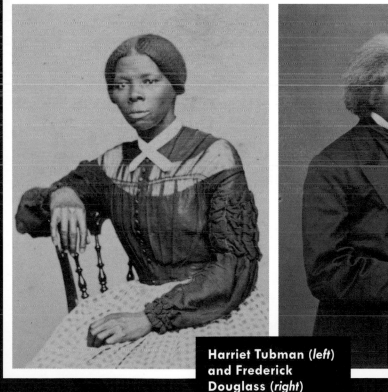

Harriet Tubman (*left*) and Frederick Douglass (*right*)

Jermain Wesley Loguen

Jermain Wesley Loguen, born into slavery in Tennessee, was once called the King of the Underground Railroad. He escaped to freedom on horseback. After escaping, he became one the most active agents on the Underground Railroad.

Not all enslaved people escaped by the Underground Railroad. Henry "Box" Brown was an enslaved man who shipped himself to freedom. In 1848 Brown's wife and children were sold, so he decided to escape. With the help of Samuel Alexander Smith, a white man, Brown shipped himself in a box on a twenty-seven-hour journey to freedom.

After escaping to freedom in the North, Black people found new challenges. Segregation and discrimination existed even where slavery didn't. Many formerly enslaved people could not read, write, or do skilled work, so they found it hard to make a living.

Then the Fugitive Slave Act of 1850 passed. The act meant that slave hunters could enter free states, capture enslaved people who had found freedom, and return them to the South. As a result, many free Black people were kidnapped, and more escaped people fled farther north to Canada.

From 1861 to 1865, the North (the Union) and the South (the Confederacy) fought each other in the Civil War. The Union wanted to end slavery. Eleven states in the South had seceded from the Union and formed the Confederate States of America to keep slavery. Black people, including those enslaved, fought in the Civil War and continued to resist.

SOUTHBOUND ROUTE TO FREEDOM

Enslaved people also escaped and went farther south for freedom. From the 1830s to 1863, an estimated three to five thousand enslaved people escaped to Mexico. Many escaped by horseback.

Mexico began to abolish slavery after gaining independence from Spain in 1821. According to historians, some enslaved people viewed Mexican troops as liberators, and many Mexicans supported the enslaved.

FREEDOM'S JOURNAL.

"RIGHTEOUSNESS EXALTETH A NATION."

NEW-YORK, FRIDAY, MARCH 30, 1827. [VOL. I. No. 3.

The *Freedom's Journal* was the first Black-owned newspaper in the US.

Being now master of a small covered boat of about 12 tons burthen, he hired a person to assist as a seaman, and made many advantageous voyages to different parts of the state of Connecticut and when about 25 years old married a native of the country, a descendant of the tribe to which his mother belonged.—— For some time after his marriage he attended chiefly to his agricultural concerns, but from an increase of family he at length deemed it necessary to pursue his commercial plans more extensively than he had before done.—— He arranged his affairs for a new expedition and hired a small house on West-Port river to which he removed his family. A boat of 16 tons was now procured in which he sailed to the banks of St. George in quest of Cod-fish and returned home with a valuable cargo. This important adventure was the foundation of an extensive & profitable fishing establishment from Westport river, which continued for a considerable time and was the source of an honest and comfortable living to many of the inhabitants of that district.

At this period Paul formed a connexion with his brother-in-law Michael Warner, who had several sons well qualified for the sea service, four of whom have since laudably filled responsible situations as Captains and first mates. A vessel of 25 tons was built, and in two voyages to the Straits of Belisle and Newfoundland he met with such success as

od. It is not so much a right of property, as it is a legal relation; and it ought to be treated as such.

The second object was, to relieve slave-holders from a charge, or an apprehension of criminality, where in fact, there is no offence. There can be no palliation for the conduct of those who first brought the curse of slavery upon poor Africa, and poor America too.—— But the body of the present generation are not liable to this charge. Posterity are not answerable for the sins of their fathers, unless they approve their deeds. They found the blacks among them, in a degraded state, incapable either of appreciating or enjoying liberty. They have, therefore, nothing to answer for on this score, because they have no other alternative, at present, but to keep them in subjection. There is nothing so demeaning by our principles, to the acknowledgment of guilt, in that which we at the same time believe to be absolutely unavoidable, and in which therefore, it is impossible really to feel self-reproach. Our southern brethren have high ideas of liberty.

There is nothing so calculated to make men restive under command, as a habit and love of commanding others. Upon their own principles, they have been forced to acknowledge even the existence of slavery, in any shape, as criminal. They have therefore concluded that as heavy a curse hung over

ance. We may hope to enjoy the favor of our merciful heavenly Father. But this is not done. I think I may venture to assert, that most of the slave-holding states, neither the laws, nor public opinion, secure to the slaves any of the privileges of humanity. Nothing more is done for them, in kind, than is done for the domestic beasts; and nothing more in degree, except as they are a more valuable species of property, and are recognised, to some extent, as possessing rational faculties. Let the contrary be shown. I say that of all that kind of provision, which goes to purify and elevate the character, and to create in the subject affection and confidence towards the government, every trace and track is completely excluded. The culture of their minds, the preservation of their morals, their instruction in the only religion which can make them good servants, happy neighbors, and hopeful heirs of eternal life, every thing of the kind is guarded against, by the laws at least, even more studiously than the abuse of their persons, and the destruction of their lives. Whatever is attempted for their improvement is done by individual effort, and in direct violation of the laws. Here is our guilt; our full, dark, unmitigated guilt. It is the guilt of our nation. We in the non-slave holding states, do not feel it as we ought. But we cannot wash our hands, until we can safely declare, that we have done every thing we can, by public and

retarded; and that the same prejudice will continue to have a similar operation, so long as it shall continue to exist. Not that there are wanting men of humanity among our West Indian legislators. Their humanity is discernable enough when it is to be applied to the *whites*; but such is the system of slavery, and the degradation attached to slavery, that their humanity seems to be lost or gone, when it is to be applied to the *blacks*. Not again that there are wanting men of sense among the same body. They are shrewd and clever enough in the affairs of life, where they maintain an intercourse with the *whites*; but in their intercourse with the *blacks* their sense appears to be shrivelled and not of its ordinary size. Look at the laws of their own making, as far as the blacks are concerned, and they are a collection of any thing but wisdom."† If these remarks are not applicable to the slave laws of our own states, let the contrary be shown.

See Ep. vi. 5, 9. Col. iii. 22. iv. 1.

† "Thoughts on the necessity of improving the condition of the slaves, &c. with a view to their ultimate emancipation." p. 10, 11.

(To be Continued)

CURE FOR DRUNKENNESS.

In speaking, on a former occasion, of the remedy for intemperance proposed by Dr.

CHAPTER 4
JUST THE BEGINNING

IN THE 1800S THE ABOLITIONIST MOVEMENT HELPED TO END SLAVERY IN THE UNITED STATES. Abolitionists worked to abolish slavery and emancipate enslaved people.

Newspapers and other print sources helped spread awareness of the abolitionist cause. The *Liberator*, started by white abolitionist William Lloyd Garrison, was the most influential antislavery newspaper. But Black people also founded significant antislavery newspapers. These included the *Mirror of Liberty*, the *Freedom's Journal*, the *National Watchman*, and the *North Star*. Narratives of slavery also played a large part in abolition. Frederick Douglass, Solomon Northup, Sojourner Truth, and more wrote about their lives as enslaved people.

The abolitionist movement influenced many other social movements, including women's rights. Just as rebellions and

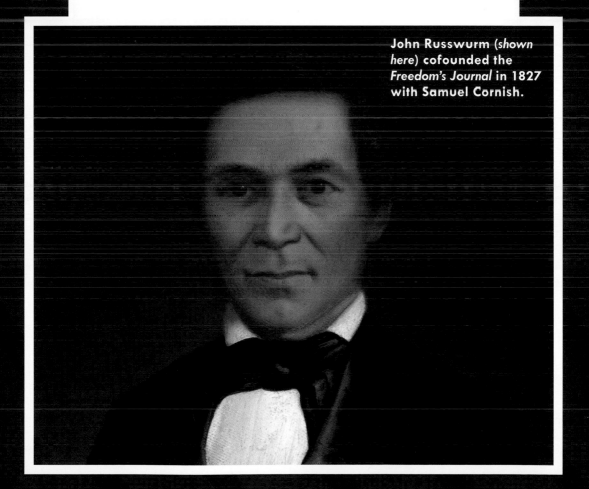

John Russwurm (*shown here*) cofounded the *Freedom's Journal* in 1827 with Samuel Cornish.

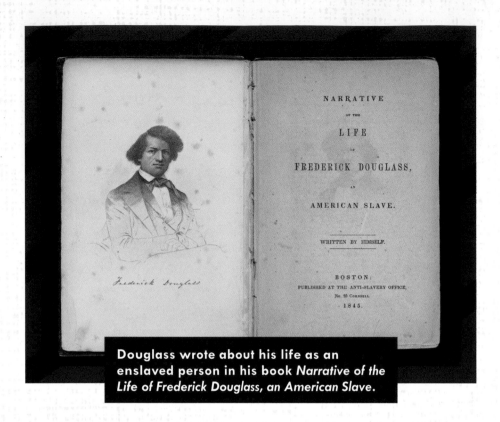

Douglass wrote about his life as an enslaved person in his book *Narrative of the Life of Frederick Douglass, an American Slave.*

REFLECT

Why do you think the written accounts of slavery are so important?

resistance fueled the abolitionist movement, the fight against segregation and racism fueled the civil rights movement in the 1950s and 1960s.

The harmful effects of slavery are still present in society. Activists and others continue to speak out against racism and discrimination. People share stories of change via social media, music, and other platforms. Anti-racist books saw a huge increase in sales in 2020 due to the Black Lives Matter movement and police brutality protests.

People protest police violence and demand racial justice at the August 28, 2020, March on Washington.

PRIMARY SOURCE VOICES

Enslaved people sometimes sang songs called spirituals. One purpose of singing spirituals was to help communicate with one another. These songs contained hidden messages that would help enslaved people run away to freedom.

Scan these QR codes to hear spirituals sung and to hear the experience of a newly freed enslaved person. While you listen, consider the words of the songs and the emotion of the singers. Why are these songs important?

https://www.loc.gov/item/jukebox-4649
A male vocal quartet performs "Steal Away," recorded on October 29, 1902.

https://www.loc.gov/item/jukebox-11026
A male vocal double quartet performs "Go Down
Moses," recorded on August 31, 1914.

Harriet Tubman was nicknamed Moses for her success
at bringing enslaved people to freedom. What message
do you think is conveyed in "Go Down Moses"?

https://www.loc.gov/item/afc1941016_afs05497a/
Laura Smalley, Hempstead, Texas, 1941

You can also follow along with the words of the
speaker in the transcript linked below the audio clip.

TAKE ACTION

Resistance is powerful and can bring about change. You can resist mistreatment and racism and fight for freedom in many ways:

Stay educated about issues. Read books and watch the news so that you can be informed about what is going on in the world.

Browse the exhibits of the National Museum of African American History & Culture online. Read about each exhibit, and see photos of items from the exhibits at https://nmaahc.si.edu/explore/exhibitions.

Write letters to your senator, governor, or any elected official. Tell them about issues that matter to you, and ask them what they are doing to help.

Talk to an adult you trust about issues that are troubling you. Talk about how you might help people who are mistreated.

Look at *The African-American Mosaic* collection by the Library of Congress to learn more about abolitionism at https://www.loc.gov/exhibits/african/afam007.html.

Check out the Read Woke Reading List on page 30 to learn more about resistance to slavery.

GLOSSARY

abolish: to get rid of or do away with

abuse: to use or treat in a way that is wrong or harmful

discrimination: unfair treatment of a particular group of people

emancipate: to free from slavery or other forms of control

influential: having the power to affect another person

mutiny: an open rebellion against authorities

rebellion: an armed fight or act of disobeying a government or ruler

resistance: the fight against or the refusal to accept or follow something

restriction: the limitation or control of someone or something

secede: to leave a group

segregation: a legal system of forced separation, done specifically by race

SOURCE NOTES

4   "Trailer: Introducing '1619,'" *New York Times*, updated September 4, 2019, https://www.nytimes.com/2019 /08/22/podcasts/1619-trailer.html.

7   John Burnett, "A Chapter in U.S. History Often Ignored: The Flight of Runaway Slaves to Mexico," National Public Radio, February 28, 2021, https://www .npr.org/2021/02/28/971325620/a-chapter-in-u-s -history-often-ignored-the-flight-of-runaway-slaves -to-mexico.

10   "Born in Slavery: Slave Narratives from the Federal Writers' Project, 1936 to 1938," Library of Congress, accessed March 29, 2021, https://www.loc.gov /collections/slave-narratives-from-the-federal -writers-project-1936-to-1938/articles-and-essays /voices-and-faces-from-the-collection/.

READ WOKE READING LIST

Atlantic Slave Trade Facts for Kids
https://kids.kiddle.co/Atlantic_slave_trade

Frederick Douglass National Historic Site
https://www.nps.gov/frdo/index.htm

Grady, Cynthia. *Like a Bird: The Art of the American Slave Song*. Minneapolis: Millbrook Press, 2016.

Hubbard, Rita L. *The Oldest Student: How Mary Walker Learned to Read*. New York: Schwartz & Wade Books, 2020.

Resistance to Slavery
http://slaveryandremembrance.org/articles/article/?id=A0006

Slave Rebellions
https://kids.britannica.com/kids/article/slave-rebellions/632865

Tyner, Dr. Artika R. *Black Lives Matter: From Hashtag to the Streets*. Minneapolis: Lerner Publications, 2021.

Weatherford, Carole Boston. *Box: Henry Brown Mails Himself to Freedom*. Somerville, MA: Candlewick, 2020.

INDEX

PHOTO ACKNOWLEDGMENTS

Image credits: Sydney King/National Park Service, p. 4; North Wind Picture Archives/Alamy Stock Photo, p. 5; National Archives, p. 6; Julian Leshay/Shutterstock.com, p. 7; Library of Congress, pp. 8, 9, 17; Smithsonian National Museum of African American History and Culture, pp. 11, 22; South Carolina Department of Archives and History, Columbia, South Carolina, p. 12; Jason O. Watson/historical-markers.org/Alamy Stock Photo, p. 13; agefotostock/Alamy Stock Photo, p. 14; Painting by Nathaniel Jocelyn/New Haven Colony Historical Society via Wikipedia Commons, p. 15; Painting by Charles T. Webber/Cincinnati Art Museum via Wikipedia Commons, p. 16; National Museum of African American History and Culture shared with the Library of Congress, p. 17 (left); History and Art Collection/Alamy Stock Photo, p. 18; Wikimedia Commons PD, p. 20; National Portrait Gallery, Smithsonian Institution, p. 21; Julian Leshay/Shutterstock.com, p. 23. Cecily Lewis portrait photos by Fernando Decillis.

Cover: Corbis/Getty Images.

Content consultant credit: Cleopatra Warren, Ph.D., Secondary History Teacher, Atlanta Public Schools, Atlanta, GA

Lerner Publications Company
An imprint of Lerner Publishing Group, Inc.
241 First Avenue North
Minneapolis, MN 55401 USA

For reading levels and more information, look up this title at www.lernerbooks.com.

Main body text set in Aptifer Sans LT Pro.
Typeface provided by Linotype AG.

Editor: Brianna Kaiser **Designer:** Viet Chu **Photo Editor:** Cynthia Zemlicka
Lerner team: Martha Kranes

Library of Congress Cataloging-in-Publication Data

Names: Lewis, Cicely, author.
Title: Resistance to slavery : from escape to everyday rebellion / Cicely Lewis.
Description: Minneapolis : Lerner Publications, [2022] | Series: American slavery and the fight
    for freedom (Read woke books) | Includes bibliographical references and index. | Audience:
    Ages: 9–14 | Audience: Grades: 4–6 | Summary: "In addition to slave uprisings and escapes
    on the Underground Railroad, enslaved people also resisted their mistreatment through
    small acts in their everyday lives. Discover the many forms of resistance to slavery"—
    Provided by publisher.
Identifiers: LCCN 2021010480 (print) | LCCN 2021010481 (ebook) | ISBN 9781728439068 (library
    binding) | ISBN 9781728444307 (ebook)
Subjects: LCSH: Slave insurrections—United States—History—Juvenile literature. | Antislavery
    movements—United States—History—Juvenile literature. | Slaves—United States—Social
    conditions—Juvenile literature. | Slavery—United States—History—Juvenile literature.
Classification: LCC E441 .L49 2022 (print) | LCC E441 (ebook) | DDC 306.3/620973—dc23

LC record available at https://lccn.loc.gov/2021010480
LC ebook record available at https://lccn.loc.gov/2021010481

Manufactured in the United States of America
1-49783-49655-8/9/2021